URBAN GARDENING AND FARMING FOR TEENS™

RAISING CHICKENS

HARVEST YOUR OWN FRESH EGGS

BRIDGET HEOS

ROSEN
PUBLISHING®

New York

Published in 2014 by The Rosen Publishing Group, Inc.
29 East 21st Street, New York, NY 10010

Copyright © 2014 by The Rosen Publishing Group, Inc.

First Edition

Library of Congress Cataloging-in-Publication Data

Heos, Bridget.
Raising chickens: harvest your own fresh eggs/Bridget Heos.—1st ed.
        p. cm.—(Urban gardening and farming for teens)
ISBN 978-1-4777-1779-0 (library binding)
1. Chickens. I. Title. II. Series: Urban gardening and farming for teens.
SF487.H445 2014
636.5—dc23

                                                                    2013018676

Manufactured in the United States of America

CPSIA Compliance Information: Batch #W14YA: For further information, contact Rosen Publishing, New York, New York, at

1-800-237-9932.

Contents

Introduction

There was something different about the chicken soup served at the MultiFaith Harvest Festival in Toledo, Ohio, in October of 2009. The chicken pieces were meatier and had more flavor. The chefs had used chickens raised by a local youth group, Toledo Grows, which provides job training to at-risk teens. Although they were raised in the city, the chickens were given room to roam and forage on an urban farm.

The teens involved learned valuable farming and work skills. Rob McCreary, eighteen, fed the chickens—which included layers (egg chickens) and broilers (meat chickens) three times a day. He said that while the work wasn't difficult, it was a learning experience, and the meat, which he enjoyed at a community barbeque, was the freshest he had tasted.

McCreary is one of many teens raising chickens in towns large and small. In Saginaw County, Michigan, 4-H members Averi Sue Copes, thirteen, and Amy Hamilton, seventeen, sought donations so that they could each raise ten chickens to donate to a local soup kitchen in town. The meat they were able to give totaled 1,000 pounds (454 kilograms). And outside of Denver, Shelby Grebenc, thirteen, raises free-range chickens to meet a demand for free-range, farm-fresh eggs and meat.

Naomi Geffken, thirteen, helps her neighbor raise chickens in Boston. She is part of the urban farming movement, which includes raising small animals for food.

Teens across America, Canada, and other countries are raising chickens to gain work experience, to get involved in their communities, or, quite simply, to put delicious food on the table. In some cases, they are rebelling against a system that favors unhealthy and factory-farmed food. Raising chickens, and the larger urban farming movement, allows teens to earn money and learn new skills, while producing fresh and healthy food.

Most teens say that raising chickens isn't particularly difficult and costs much less than raising other farm animals (each broiler cost the 4-H girls $6 to raise). It does take time, consistent work, and a willingness to learn as you go. And if you plan to sell your eggs, it will take a little hard-nosed business sense, too. Shelby Grebenc says people are always trying to talk her down on prices. But she tells people that her eggs taste better because they come from free-range chickens and are worth the price.

If you are interested in raising your own chickens, either as a source of eggs for your family and friends or as a business, read on to learn how to get started and grow your urban farm.

CHAPTER ONE

BRIGHT LIGHTS, LITTLE CITY FARMS

Since the Agricultural Revolution ten thousand years ago, people have grown and raised food on the land where they live. With the Industrial Revolution beginning in the 1700s, many people in Europe and America moved from rural areas to cities. They worked in factories and lived in small, crowded houses and buildings called tenements. Some city dwellers raised chickens and small farm animals, but with so little space and sunlight, most could no longer grow their own food. They had to buy it instead.

Through the years there were sometimes efforts to farm urban lots, to cope with food shortages during World War II, for instance. Today, urban gardens are cropping up on rooftops, vacant lots, and yards. They are combating new problems, such as food deserts, factory farms, and a sedentary lifestyle. Teens who have joined the movement have gained new independence, knowledge, and fresh food for themselves and their families.

While many urban gardeners focus on growing fruits, vegetables, and herbs, there is also a way to raise animals in the city.

The Industrial Revolution brought droves of people to cities like New York (pictured here in 1895). Lack of land and sunlight made raising animals and growing food a thing of the past for many people.

Because of the small space they require, chickens are the city livestock of choice for many urban farmers. You'll learn how to raise chickens and harvest eggs. But first, here is a little background on why other teens are joining the urban gardening movement by raising chickens.

A LACK OF FRESH, HEALTHY FOOD IN URBAN NEIGHBORHOODS

According to the Web site the Week, 23.5 million Americans live in a food desert, defined as an area where at least 20 percent of people live under the poverty line, and 33 percent live a mile (1.6 kilometers) away from a supermarket (or 10 miles [16 km] away in rural areas). This can lead residents to rely on high-fat and low-nutrition food from fast food restaurants and convenience stores. Growing produce or raising animals in their backyards provides teens with nutritious food regardless of their neighborhood resources. In the morning, they can gather eggs and cook them for their family in less time than it would take to drive through a fast food restaurant for breakfast for one.

PIGS (AND GOATS, RABBITS, AND DUCKS) IN THE CITY

Besides chickens, these other farm animals are sometimes raised in the city.

Goats. Goats are raised as pets, for milk, or both. They require more room than chickens (135 square feet [13 square meters] for a miniature, and you'll need to keep two since they are herd animals). Also, for them to produce milk, they need to be bred and have babies. They can live up to fifteen years.

Pot-bellied pigs. While hogs are raised for meat, these small pigs (which can grow to 130 pounds [59 kg]) are kept as pets. Much like a dog, they require food, shelter, companionship, space to run, and walks.

Rabbits. Rabbits are raised as pets, but also for meat. Like chickens, they take up little space and are generally allowed in cities.

Ducks. Ducks are raised for eggs and meat. They require much the same care as chickens. They tend to be better layers, but can be messier and noisier than chickens. Ducks also need more water than chickens, though the amount varies by breed.

AN ANSWER TO URBAN BLIGHT

Urban gardens are not only helpful to teens and their families, but to the whole neighborhood, as they cut down on urban blight (which in turn cuts down on crime). When people convert vacant or unused land to garden space, it becomes useful. Useful land is looked after, and looked after land is beautiful. Studies have

Capitol Hill residents in Washington, D.C., work in a community garden in 2010. Community gardens bring people together and allow them to grow nutritious food in the city.

shown that rundown property attracts crime, whereas cared-for property does the opposite. Also, when people are outside tending gardens or animals, they talk to each other and keep an eye on things. This builds friendship and community. As urban gardens expand, neighbors share or trade produce, expanding their choices of fresh food.

TO GET OUTSIDE

Another reason teens are joining the urban gardening movement is to get outdoors. The American Academy of Pediatrics recommends that kids and teens spend an hour outside each day for optimal physical and mental health. But in reality, the Nature

Conservancy reports that only 6 percent of children play outside on their own in a typical day. On the other hand, children average more than seven hours a day on entertainment media—practically all of their free time after school. With 80 percent of the U.S. population living in urban areas, according to the *San Francisco Chronicle*, it's not surprising that teens have lost touch with the natural world. The proportion of children ages nine through twelve who spent time hiking, fishing, walking, playing on the beach, or gardening, declined 50 percent between 1997 and 2003. Urban gardening gets teens back in touch with the natural world and teaches them how to rely on nature for food. As with any skill, once they master one aspect of urban gardening, other skills start to make sense. For instance, you may start by raising chickens for eggs. Soon, you see that you can raise vegetables, too. Now, you can make a full breakfast of omelets for your family.

TO STEP OUTSIDE THE INDUSTRIAL FOOD SYSTEM

Some teens have begun raising food out of concern about the modern industrial food system. In regard to chickens, there is concern for sanitation and humane treatment of the birds. Factory farm chickens are crowded into cages or indoor barns and often crippled by the wire floors. Their beaks are removed so that they don't cannibalize each other, a painful process. Their eggs suffer because of this stressful life, and bacteria can spread because of overcrowding. In August 2010, the U.S. Food and Drug Administration (FDA) recalled half a billion eggs for salmonella poisoning. *Consumer Reports* tested supermarket broilers and found that 66 percent were contaminated with salmonella or campylobacter, according to *The Small-Scale Poultry Flock*.

These bacteria can cause food poisoning, a condition that not only causes nausea, but can have long-term health effects. Even eggs and meat labeled "free-range chickens" are not necessarily free range. There are no regulations on the use of the term for egg chickens and "free-range" meat chickens are only required by the U.S. Department of Agriculture (USDA) to spend some (any amount of) time outdoors.

In more general terms, the modern food industry relies on the transportation of products, which leads to carbon emissions that contribute to global warming. Large-scale fertilization of crops pollutes waterways and also contributes to global warming. Raising your own food cuts down on carbon emissions released when transporting food. And on a small scale, you can also use fertilizer (chicken manure) in a way that is sustainable and beneficial to the soil.

JOIN THE MOVEMENT

If you're interested in raising chickens, you must first decide if you can raise them at home. First, do you have enough space? Urban dwellers have raised chickens in their yards, on vacant lots, and even on rooftops. Chickens don't require a great deal of room, but they do need a coop and small run. Each bird needs 4 square feet (.4 square meters) inside the coop, and 10 square feet (.9 square meters) outside. Chickens are social animals, so you should keep at least two at a time. A 3-by-3 foot (1 m-by-1 m) coop and a 4-by-5 foot (1.2 m-by-1.5 m) run for two birds would be enough space.

You'll also need to check the rules and regulations regarding chickens in your town or city. You may be surprised to learn that many big cities, including New York, allow chickens. In some cities and towns, there are limits on the number of birds you can have or the distance they must be from a neighbor's property. If your town doesn't allow chickens, you can lobby your local government to change the rules, though that will take time. Even if you are allowed to have chickens, you should talk to your neighbors. They may have a laid-back attitude about chickens. However, they may be concerned about the noise and chicken droppings. Assure them that the chickens will be well cared for and cooped up at night, that the manure will be managed responsibly, and that chickens, as a rule, are not very loud. (This is also a good introduction if you'd like to sell your eggs to neighbors).

A couple of final considerations: if you have allergies or asthma, the feathers and dust associated with chickens can exacerbate symptoms. Talk to your doctor, as raising chickens may not be a good fit for you, and you should opt for another form of urban gardening instead. If you have a pet, consider its temperament. Some dogs and cats can learn to accept other animals as "not to eat." Your dog may even guard chickens, while a cat can control rodents attracted to chicken feed and eggs. On the other hand, if your pet has an uncontrollable killer instinct, chickens would obviously not be a good fit. Also, other people's dogs and cats will not view your chickens as part of the family and should be kept away.

Meghan Ryan, twenty-four, raises chickens Camilla, Franny, and Enid in Brooklyn, New York. Rules on raising chickens in the city vary; in many places they are allowed.

If you are able to raise chickens at home, educate yourself and find support. You can start by reading books and reaching out to others who raise chickens. You may have an older relative or neighbor who grew up caring for chickens and can offer advice. The owner of a feed store may know a chicken farmer you could talk to. Online forums provide a space for chicken raisers to ask and answer questions. Programs like 4-H can also offer education and support. 4-H is a youth organization that includes animal husbandry programs. Though traditionally associated with rural areas, 4-H is growing in cities. Finally, college extensions offer information regarding farming and raising animals.

If you are unable to raise chickens at home, you still have options:

- Help a neighbor or join an urban farming group or youth group that is already raising chickens. Offer to help in exchange for eggs.
- Encourage your church, school, or community garden to add a chicken program.
- Ask your science teacher if you can raise chickens as a class project on school property.

CHAPTER TWO

GETTING STARTED

Once you've decided to raise chickens, it's time to set goals and a budget. Do you plan to raise chickens only to have eggs for your family? Will you sell some eggs to pay for expenses? Will you have a full-scale egg selling operation? Will you breed the chickens in order to sell chicks to schools or other farmers?

Next, make a budget. Write down what you need to raise chickens, and estimate the cost. You can buy female chicks for about $2.75 each. (The company may require a minimum order, though). A 5-pound (2.3 kg) bag of chick feed will cost about $10. A chick feeder and water fountain together will cost about $20. A heat lamp costs about $20. For housing, you can use a cardboard box to start with. You can make your own bedding, although wood chips work best. Raising chicks could cost about $70 to start, in addition to the cost of feed and a larger coop later. To cut down on costs, you can check Web sites for used supplies, or try freecycle.com. Just don't cut corners at the expense of the chicks' health. For instance,

Nichole Devorss gets chicks ready for sale at a farm supply store in Sedalia, Mo. Chicks can be purchased in stores or markets, or ordered online for delivery by mail.

a chick feeder is more sanitary than a bowl, so it keeps the chicks healthier. They'll require fewer trips to the vet. In the long run, a chick feeder is cost effective (not to mention it results in happier chicks).

One dozen farm-fresh eggs sell for about $3. With three hens, you'll get about two eggs a day, or fourteen in a week. Say you sell two dozen a month to a neighbor and keep the rest. You'll earn $6 a month to help pay for chicken feed, or $72 per year. Plus, you have your own eggs and don't have to buy them at the store, which could save $72 per year. Of course, the hens won't lay eggs right away. They need to grow up first. And in addition to your $70 in startup expenses, your chicken feed expenses are ongoing. In other words, you won't get rich raising chickens. You may only break even. But you'll learn a lot and will have fresh food right in your backyard.

Let's talk more about what you'll need to get started. The chicks can start their lives in a small box. They each need half a square foot (465 square centimeters) of space from the time they are one day to four weeks old and then an additional square foot each month until they are pullets (young chickens). The sides should be 18 inches high (46 cm) so that they don't escape. (They wouldn't go far, but away from the heat lamp, they could get cold). Line the box with soft bedding, such as wood chips or strips of paper. If you have a cat or dog, cover the box with a screen. Have medicated chick feed on hand because the chicks will need to eat as soon as they come home. They'll also need grit, which you'll sprinkle in their box to encourage exercise and help with digestion.

SAVE THE HEIRLOOM CHICKENS!

Did you know that almost one-third of chicken breeds are close to going extinct? Certain breeds have been favored by commercial chicken farms at the expense of other breeds. Maintaining the diversity of animal breeds is important because different breeds are resistant to different diseases. If only a handful of breeds thrive, a disease could wipe out a large percentage of chickens. You can help conserve dying breeds by choosing from the American Livestock Breeds Conservancy's Conservation Priority List. You can also serve a niche market of customers who want heirloom eggs. Here are some heritage breeds:

Brahmas are large chickens (hens can reach 14 pounds [6 kg]) with feathered legs and feet. They are docile, easily kept in coops and pens, and hardy in cold climates. However, the hens tend to get broody. (They feel the need to sit on eggs, even if they're unfertilized. The hen will not lay new eggs during this time.)

Dominiques were brought to America by the Pilgrims. They do well in urban henhouses.

Orpingtons are among the more docile breeds of chickens. Quiet and calm, they'll eat from their owner's hands. If your neighbors are wary of chickens, they won't likely complain about these sweet heirloom chickens.

The next question is: where do you get chickens? One option is to buy fertilized eggs and incubate them. More commonly, people order chicks by mail. They survive up to three days en route because, while in the egg, they absorbed enough nutrition to last that long. If you are only raising chickens for eggs, you'll

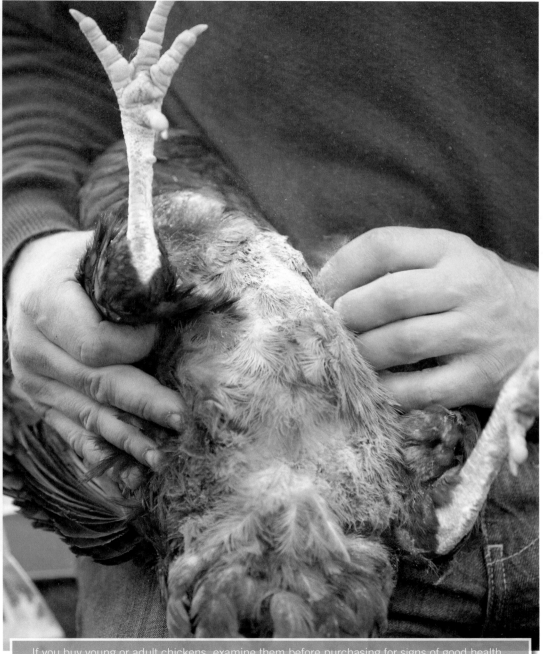

If you buy young or adult chickens, examine them before purchasing for signs of good health. Look for full, healthy feathers, well-scaled legs, a straight breast bone, a scar-free comb, and bright eyes.

want to buy sexed (female only) chicks. Otherwise, your chicks will include males. Roosters tend to be noisy and are not needed for egg-laying operations. They are best raised on rural farms.

You can also buy young or full-grown hens from breeders. The National Poultry Improvement Plan has a directory of hatcheries and breeders that test their poultry for diseases. You can also have a veterinarian check their health. Look for a full, blemish-free comb. Abnormal combs can mean disease; scars can mean aggressiveness. Their eyes should be bright and clear and their noses not runny. Their breast bone should be straight and well-feathered, their legs well-scaled and smooth. Check under their wattles and wings for parasites.

Next, decide which breeds to raise.

CHOOSING A BREED

Breeds vary in terms of docility (calmness,) flightiness (meaning easily scared, so that when they are approached, they run or fly away), assertiveness or aggressiveness, and resourcefulness (some birds will strive to stay cool on hot days by moving into the shade, for instance, while others suffer because they simply can't adapt). Their needs vary, too. Some breeds need more space and food than others. Heavy feathered birds, such as Faverolles, Orpingtons, Chanteclers, and Silkies, do well in cold climates, whereas lighter feathered birds are hot-weather hardy. Finally, egg size, color, and productivity vary by breed. Eggs tend to be white or brown, but they can be a variety of shades, from tan to chocolate and from green tinted to cream. The Ameraucana lays eggs that are pale green, blue, and pink and for this reason is known as the Easter egg hen. While brown

The Ameraucana chicken is known as the Easter egg chicken because of its pastel green, blue, and pink eggs. The hens are active but quiet and calm.

eggs are no healthier than white eggs, some people associate brown with farm freshness, so if you plan to sell your eggs, you may opt to raise chickens that lay brown eggs. Interestingly, hens with white earlobes tend to lay white eggs, whereas hens with red earlobes lay brown eggs.

Within each breed, chickens come in various colors and sizes. Many breeds have mini versions called bantams. These chickens are good for small spaces but are more susceptible to bad weather and lay smaller eggs. And while some breeds are known for either their sweet or bossy demeanor, each chicken has its own personality. Chick companies will likely allow you to choose chicks from a variety of breeds. Just don't mix especially bossy breeds with docile breeds, as the calmer chickens could get bullied. Here are some descriptions of chicken breeds:

Silkie bantams are white, furry-looking chickens. They do well in confinement and in many climates.

Australorps are sweet chickens that lay a lot of eggs. You shouldn't raise domineering breeds alongside Australorps, which tend to get bullied.

Brahmas are big and gentle. They do well in colder climates and are happier as free-range chickens.

Plymouth/Barred Rocks are black-and-white chickens that can be happy in a fenced pen or pasture. They lay brown eggs.

Rhode Island Reds are the dark red chickens that you often see in art. Boisterous and vocal, they are great egg producers, but they need space to forage, such as a large yard or pasture.

Ameraucanas (Easter egg hens) are known for their beautiful green, blue, and pink eggs. They are active like Rhode Island Reds, but quieter and calmer.

True to their name, Jersey Giants can grow to 11 pounds (5 kg) and lay large eggs. The eggs can be brown, cream, or speckled. These large hens need space and are slow to mature. However, they are kind to their handlers and tend to get along with other breeds.

Welsummers are independent and known for their beautiful chocolate-colored eggs. The roosters of this breed are the dark red and blue roosters often depicted in art and advertisements.

CHAPTER THREE

CARING FOR CHICKS AND PULLETS

Domestic chickens are descended from the jungle fowl of Asian and Pacific forests. In the wild, they live in groups of about twelve and come home to the same roost every night. They can fly better than domestic breeds. Roosters crow at dawn and are feisty but protective of hens and chicks. Hens raise their chicks, teaching them to eat and drink, and keep them warm. Domesticated chickens behave in much the same way.

If you start out raising chicks, you'll need to provide everything their mother would provide. You'll keep them warm and teach them to eat and drink. For both hens and chicks, you'll provide the protection that a rooster would provide in the wild.

Chicks should be kept inside at first. Their box needs soft bedding, such as pine shavings or strips of paper. It should be kept dry and warm—hot actually. The first week the chicks come home, the box should register 95 degrees Fahrenheit (35 degrees Celsius). This can be achieved by hanging a 250-watt

Roosters are not needed for egg-laying operations and are not recommended for urban farms because of their noisiness and boisterous behavior. However, they are spectacular birds to behold.

heat lamp 17 inches (43 cm) from the bottom of the pen. You can attach it with a clip to a board over the box. Each week, decrease the heat by 5 degrees (by moving the lamp higher above the box) until their space registers 70°F (21°C). The box should be in a fairly quiet place. However, you should handle your chicks daily so that they learn not to fear you. You can also sing to the chicks to relax them, which is what mother hens do.

Use a regulation chick feeder and water fount. These prevent droppings from contaminating the food and water. You'll still need to provide fresh water and scoop the poop out of the feeder twice a day, as chicks are messy. Clean the entire box every four days. About once a week, you may want to replace the box with a bigger box.

When they first arrive, dip each chick's nose into the water to show them where to drink. Make sure each chick takes a drink of water. Next, do the same with the food. Provide the chicks with medicated chick feed to keep them disease-free (although chicks may still become sick). Make sure all the chicks

pen can be kept outside. At this age, the pullets shouldn't be exposed to nighttime temperatures lower than 60°F (16°C). If it's still cold during the day, acclimate the pullets by bringing them outside for a couple of sunny hours each day.

The permanent pen should be large enough to provide each chicken with 3 square feet (.3 square m). It should allow air circulation, but windows should be screened to keep out predators, and the door should have a latch. If rodents or digging animals (like foxes) are a problem, the coop will need a floor—solid not wire, which can hurt the chickens' feet. Alternately, a wire fence can be buried below ground level. Other than that, you can get creative with the coop. Buying new can be expensive—$200 for the most basic model. Buying used is cheaper. Search online or ask other urban gardeners if they know of sellers. You can also build your own chicken coop, either starting from scratch with new or recycled materials or by converting an old doghouse, playhouse, or shed into a chicken coop.

The coop should open to a run, a fenced-in space in which your chickens can peck and roam during the day. You may also allow them free range. On a farm, they may be able to roam freely all day because there are plenty of places to hide from predators. However, they'll still need to be locked safely in the coop at night, when predators are a greater threat. You can train them to come home to roost. After they're acclimated to the new coop, start letting them out late in the afternoon so that they come back by evening. Gradually let them out earlier.

In the city, free range is not really an option. You can let them roam while you're there to supervise. But if they're given the

RAISING A GARDEN ALONGSIDE CHICKENS

Chickens can be helpers in the garden. They'll eliminate pests by hunting for slugs and insects. They'll be the cleanup crew for fallen fruit. And they'll provide powerful fertilizer in the form of their manure.

Likewise, a garden can keep your chickens happy and healthy. Chickens enjoy nibbling on blackberry nightshade, black wattle, catnip, chickweed, fat-hen, ginger, nasturtium, nettles, oats, rue, and wormwood. Planting them in your garden, or in a separate area, will make foraging fun for your chickens.

run of the yard while you're not home, they may roam into other yards and bother the neighbors, or worse, be attacked by pets or strays. A pen will give most breeds the freedom they need.

If your coop is stationary, they'll likely tear up the part of the yard under the pen. This is to be expected, but dry dirt is not much fun for them. You'll need to provide scraps for them to forage. On the other hand, a mobile pen allows tractoring. The coop and pen are moved every couple days so that the chickens can forage throughout the yard. This also spreads their manure around the yard, which fertilizes the grass.

At night, lock the chickens safely in the coop. Chicken predators include large birds like hawks and owls, foxes, dogs, cats, and even rats (though they are primarily interested in eggs and

WARNING
ELECTRIC FENCE

Chickens require both a coop (here, a stone chicken house) and a run, the outdoor fenced area. In this case, the fence is electric to ward off predators.

chicken feed). If predators are raiding the coop, find out how they are entering and seal off that entrance. If the predator is crafty and continues to break in, try scaring it. Predators flee when they hear people or loud noises. You can keep them at bay by tuning an outdoor radio to talk radio (as long as it doesn't keep your neighbors awake) or by hanging pie tins on a string attached to the coop. If predators approach, the tins will make a racket.

Inside the coop, the chickens will need roosts, feeding trays, watering founts, and space for dust baths. The bedding should be 4 to 8 inches (10 to 20 cm) deep. Wood shavings are best but expensive. You can also use straw, dry lawn clippings, shredded paper, or newspaper.

YOUR GROWING PULLETS

At six weeks old, your pullets can withstand a 50°F (10°C) night. If it's cooler than that, continue to bring them inside at night. Also bring them inside if it gets hotter than 95°F (35°C). On hot days, provide shade and multiple water stations. Hose down the coop several times a day to keep it cool inside.

When they are eight weeks old, switch the hens to developer, or grower, feed, which they'll eat until they are twenty weeks old. Holding them will be harder now, but continue to handle them so that they are manageable when you need to transport them or administer medicine. To herd the pullets, hold your arms out, walking slowly, then calmly move to catch one. Hold the pullet in the crook of your arm (like a newborn baby) securing both wings so that she doesn't flap.

The pullets will continue to peck at each other. Again, this is natural chicken behavior. But extreme, or cannibalistic, pecking should be prevented or stopped. Avoid stressful situations for the hens, such as hot coops, boredom, and limited food and water stations. Make sure they are getting proper nutrition, as poor nutrition can lead to pecking. Salt deficiency can bring on excessive pecking, so if pecking is a problem, you can try adding salt to their water. Clean wounds caused by pecking, as

Hens need nesting boxes in which to lay their eggs. This is one example; you can also recycle any sturdy box, including a litter box.

chickens will go for blood if they see it. Remove injured, bullied, or bullying pullets from the flock. (It's a good idea to have a cage designated for injured, sick, or broody hens).

When the pullets are three months old, add a nesting box to your coop. You can use crates or litter boxes raised on cinder blocks. The hens will begin laying when they're about five months old. They can share a nesting box, but if you have several chickens, you may want to add two boxes. To encourage your hens to lay in the box, instead of on the ground or outside in the grass, put a fake egg in the box. At this point, your pullets will also switch to feed designed for laying chickens.

CHAPTER FOUR

RAISING LAYERS

Female chickens are pullets until they are one year old. They begin laying while still pullets. As they grow, you'll continue to feed, protect, and shelter them. Your full-grown hens can withstand colder and warmer temperatures now, but in the winter, lay an insulating blanket over the coop or add a heat lamp. To prevent frostbite, apply petroleum jelly to your hens' wattles and combs. In extreme cold, you may need to move the chickens inside. In the summer, the hens shouldn't be exposed to temperatures hotter than 95°F (35°C). Cool your yard by providing shade and water, or move the chickens inside. You can also mist the hens to cool them off.

As your hens approach egg-laying age, their nutritional needs change. Twenty-week-old pullets begin eating layer feed. This should include calcium, as eggshells leach calcium from the mother. (If the feed is not high in calcium, you can provide your hens with oyster shells as a supplement). Beyond filling the

In addition to chicken feed, scatter chicken scratch in the yard, which promotes good health and keeps the chickens busy. You can also add treats like fruits, vegetables, and yogurt.

feeder, you'll want to provide scratch, treats, and opportunities to forage.

Your feeding routine may be to let the chickens out of the coop before school and throw scratch in the yard. Scratch may include cracked corn, wheat, and oats. It keeps hens busy and helps with digestion. It can also be used to train chickens. Say "chick chick" when you throw it on the ground, and the hens will come to you when they hear this command. In the morning, you'll also change their water. After school, you'll refill their feeders and gather eggs. (It's a good idea to have more than one feeding station. That way, hens low in the pecking order will still get a turn to eat).

You may also give the chickens treats in the evening. Though chicken feed is comprised of grain, chickens are omnivores and enjoy a wide variety of foods. You can feed them meat scraps, yogurt, and vegetables such as tomatoes, corn, and lettuce. Avoid onions or garlic, as these make their eggs taste funny. Treats are especially important in cold weather, when the hens are cooped up and bored and need to be fattened up to withstand the cold. In the evening, you can give your hens the opportunity to forage in your yard. They'll search the ground for insects and weeds they like (such as dandelion leaves).

Soon your pullets will begin laying eggs. Eggs are laid through the hen's vent, the opening on her underside. First eggs are small but edible. The shells may be blood stained. By the second month, the eggs will be normal size and appear more regularly. In their first year, hens can lay up to three hundred eggs, a number that varies by breed. They'll lay up to two hundred per year for the next couple of years. Though they lay eggs for a decade, egg production decreases each year after the first few years. Hens lay eggs on an interesting schedule. Each hen lays her egg one hour later each day until dusk. Then, she lays an egg in the morning, and the process starts over.

Hens stop laying in the winter because it would be a bad time to raise chicks (the evolutionary purpose of laying eggs). Hens lay best between 45 to 80°F (7 to 27°C) and stop laying when there are less than thirteen hours of daylight. To extend the laying season, you must add artificial light—incandescent or fluorescent—to the coop in the evening. As the hours of daylight decrease, your hens will molt. Over the course of about seven weeks, they'll shed their old feathers and grow new ones. During this time, they'll lay few or no eggs. They'll also be unusually quiet and may become easily stressed out. You can help them through this time by misting them (if it is not too cold outside) to help with the shedding. Be sure they are all getting plenty of food and staying warm.

A few problems may arise with eggs. One is that a hen can become broody. This means that she wants to incubate her

SIMPLE EGG RECIPES

BOILED EGGS

Place a few eggs in a pot of cold water. Make sure the water covers the eggs by an inch or two. Bring to a boil over high heat. Remove from the heat. Cover the pot and let it sit for twelve minutes. Carefully pour out the hot water and add cold water to the pan. Once the eggs cool, they are ready to peel.

EGG IN A BASKET

Cut a circle out of the center of a slice of bread. Melt a table-spoon of butter in a frying pan over medium heat. Lay the bread in the center of the pan and the removed bread circle beside it. Crack an egg into the cut-out hole. Sprinkle with salt. Cook for 2–3 minutes. Flip the bread and egg, and cook on the other side for 1–2 minutes. (Flip the small bread circle at the same time.) Place the bread circle on top of the egg. Remove from the pan.

OMELET

Melt butter in a pan over medium heat. With a fork or whisk, beat two eggs and ¼ cup milk. Pour the mixture into the pan. Let cook for two to three minutes or until the eggs begin to solid-ify. Sprinkle cheese over half the mixture. You can add other ingredients, such as tomatoes or meat. With a spatula, lift the noncheese half of the omelet and fold it over the cheesy part. Cook for 1–2 more minutes. If the flipping doesn't work out, you can turn the omelet into scrambled eggs instead, breaking up the mixture with the spatula until it is cooked.

unfertilized eggs. During this time, she doesn't lay eggs. You can usually break this spell by removing her from the coop and placing her in the isolated cage until she forgets. However, if she

Eggs can vary in size and color, and occasionally a hen will lay an odd egg. In this case, it's a giant one. The hen's owner, Becca Kays of Montana, estimates that it is 3 by 2 inches (8 by 5 cm).

is constantly broody, you might consider selling her to a chicken breeder. Brooders are valuable because they will incubate not just their own eggs, but other fertilized eggs, as well. Second, a hen may stop laying eggs. If this happens after normal laying, and there is no apparent reason (such as molting), check with a veterinarian, as the hen may be sick or getting poor nutrition. A third problem is that a hen may become an egg eater. Chickens enjoy the taste of eggs, but egg eating should be discouraged or you won't have any eggs left to eat or sell. You'll need to remove an egg eater from the flock before others begin to copy her.

You may also get abnormal eggs. Some are nothing to worry about. Misshapen eggs, for instance, tend to be flukes most common among young and old hens. "Fart eggs"—eggs smaller than usual—are due to the shell forming around tissue inside the hen. The problem resolves itself. Within the egg, a double yolk just means that two yolks were produced at the same time. A blood spot on the yolk is merely a popped blood vessel (not an early embryo, as some people believe). Both are safe to eat. Abnormalities that could indicate problems include blood out-side the shell. This is normal when the pullet first starts laying, but later, it could mean that the hen has red mites. Your vet can prescribe medicine for this. An egg with a soft shell or no shell could mean a calcium deficiency in the hen's diet (though an occasional soft egg can be a fluke).

Sadly, you may need to cull some of your hens from the flock. Reasons include broodiness, aggressiveness, egg eating, or fail-ure to lay eggs. Typically, people cull hens by butchering them for meat. This can be a sad decision. Raising animals, it's natu-ral to become attached. But keep in mind that you gave your hens a better life than they would have had in many commercial enterprises. While you may decide to bear with a broody hen or to let an older hen who has stopped laying eggs retire in peace, in other cases, removing a problem hen is essential to the health of the flock. You can learn how to humanely butcher a hen at home or send it to a processor. The meat need not go to waste. Scald the butchered bird, shuck off the feathers, remove the neck, and bake it.

BREEDING CHICKENS

While most urban dwellers raise hens only, you may be curious about breeding chickens. In general, one rooster is sufficient for up to twelve hens (just like in the wild). He will protect the hens and help them find food. Roosters don't typically mate with all the hens. Just like humans, some roosters and hens hit it off, whereas others don't like each other at all. This means that some of your hens will continue to lay unfertilized eggs that you can eat. You'll need to observe which hens make a love connection with the rooster to ensure that their eggs are incubated. If one mother hen isn't broody, the eggs can be given to another broody hen.

Eggs incubate for about twenty-one days. If some are slow to hatch, the mother may stop brooding. You can place the eggs under a still-broody hen or in an incubator. The mother hen will care for her chicks for six weeks. She will teach them to eat and drink and keep them warm. You'll still need to keep an eye on the chicks. Even with their mother hen watching over them, pecking order can be an issue.

A mother hen protects her chicks, keeps them warm, and teaches them to eat and drink. When you own chicks, you are their mother hen and must provide the same things.

What do people do with all those chicks? They can be sold to other poultry farmers. Or the fertilized eggs can be sold to schools, which incubate them as part of the science curriculum. (You would then pick up the hatched chicks and raise or sell them). While a breeding operation requires much more time and space than a simple egg-laying project, you might want to try it for a short time to learn more about animal husbandry. If roosters are not allowed in your municipality, you may be able to borrow or rent one for this purpose.

CHAPTER FIVE

HEALTH, SANITATION, AND SAFETY

In this section, you'll learn about sanitation, health, and safety for chicken farmers and chickens. First, chicken manure, like all waste, harbors bacteria like salmonella, which can make you sick. Be sure to wash your hands after handling the chickens and their bedding, feeders, and other items. If managed properly, manure doesn't have to smell or harbor larger pests. In fact, this nitrogen-rich manure can be used or sold as fertilizer. Most people handle the bedding in the chicken coop like this: once a week, they stir the soiled bedding and then add more bedding on top of it. In the spring, they clean out the old bedding in the coop. By then, the manure has broken down and can be added to the soil. This is actually a sanitary way to manage manure. The new bedding covers up the smell while the manure underneath decomposes. While flies will lay eggs in the manure, fly predators will also make their homes in the composting manure, so you won't have a fly problem. For the chickens, the process of decomposing also releases heat throughout the winter.

These urban chickens in Los Angeles have plenty of room to roam while still staying safe in their pen from cars, wildlife, and roaming pets.

On the other hand, you may decide to fully clean the coop weekly, particularly if there is a removable tray. Either dispose of the manure or let it ferment in a separate location, still covering it to cut down on the smell. To keep the coop clean throughout the year, make sure it is well ventilated and that the bedding doesn't get too wet. Repair leaky roofs, remove damp bedding, and don't crowd too many chickens in the coop.

When you clean the coop, wear a dust mask, as manure can be irritating, especially for those with allergies. Remove the bedding and spread it about 1 inch (2.5 cm) thick on your garden before planting, or bag it up to sell to neighbors who garden. Forty-five pounds (20 kg) of manure (the amount created by one hen in a year) fertilizes 100 square feet (9 square m) of garden. Next, remove the nests, feeders, and waters. Wash these and the coop down with a solution of bleach and water. Spread new bedding in the coop. As for manure in the yard, if chickens have a wide enough range, it will be spread thin enough to fertilize the yard. However, if they use a stationary run, the manure will need to be removed weekly.

Eggs should be kept clean to avoid bacterial contamination. Keep the nests away from roosting areas so that they are not pooped on by perching birds. Throw away heavily soiled eggs. You can lightly scrub a little dirt off with a brush, but do not wash eggs with water. This washes away their protective coating and could allow bacteria to cling to the egg. As soon as you gather the eggs, refrigerate them. Don't eat foods that contain raw eggs, such as cookie dough and brownie batter. If you eat chickens culled from the flock, be sure the meat is well done.

CSI: CHICKEN SCENE INVESTIGATION

It's important to address any attack on your chickens or else the predator will return again and again. To stop a predator, you must first identify it. For instance, a fox needs to be stopped from digging under the coop, whereas a hawk must be stymied from above. Here are some of the clues different predators leave behind:

A single missing hen with a trail of feather clusters every 40 feet (12 m) or so: a fox. Foxes drag away their prey, shaking them periodically, until they reach their den or a quiet spot to eat.

A chicken carcass in the coop or pen, with all or part of the animal's entrails eaten: opossum. You might even see the opossum nearby, as they will return to eat more of their kill.

A chicken carcass in the coop or pen, with the breast meat eaten: raccoon. Raccoons tend to eat one bird at a time and go for the meaty portions.

Several chickens dead, but not eaten: a dog. Dogs kill for sport, but unless hungry, won't eat the chickens.

Spilled or eaten chicken feed and missing eggs: this is likely a rodent, which targets chicken feed, eggs, and chicks, but not typically full-grown hens. If you live in bear country, spilled chicken feed could also be the work of a bear.

A chicken attacked at the neck or missing without a trace: a hawk. A hawk will fly away with a chicken if possible. If the chicken is too heavy, the hawk will eat it on site. It tends to go for the throat and leave behind a mess of feathers.

CHICKEN HEALTH

The best way to keep chickens healthy is through preventative measures. Give chicks medicated feed and keep feeders and waterers clean to prevent coccidiosis, a common disease caused by chicks accidentally eating their droppings. Blood in droppings is a sign of coccidiosis, and chicks showing symptoms should be treated. Another common ailment among chicks is, for lack of a better term, "pasty butt." The chicks' droppings dry over their vent, making it impossible for them to poop. Check your chicks' vents daily for this condition. If they have it, wipe the dried poop off with a warm, wet washcloth. Chick raisers have several home

Good health can be promoted by avoiding overcrowding, removing overly aggressive hens from the flock, providing nutritious food, and keeping chickens comfortable in extreme climates. Still, health problems can arise.

remedies to prevent pasty butt, such as adding scrambled eggs to the diet for protein, yogurt as a probiotic, reducing the heat in the box, or adding sand to the chicks' grit. Whatever you choose to do as prevention, it's essential that you treat the actual problem. Keep the vents clean and unclogged, or their digestion will be disrupted and the chicks will become very sick. If you clean the vents daily, the condition usually clears up in a few days.

For older chickens, clean, dry coops, and stress-free living conditions go a long way to promote good health. Avoid having too many chickens. Overcrowded conditions can lead to the spread of disease. Provide dusting areas, as dust baths prevent lice and mites. Move birds around the yard or clean their run frequently so that they aren't pecking at manure. Make sure your chickens are getting proper nutrition. You can ask your vet about giving your chickens immunizations against common diseases in your area.

Even with proper care, chickens can get sick. Respiratory disease symptoms include sneezing and coughing, along with decreased egg production or quality. A vet can prescribe medication. Strange-looking eggs or sick-looking chickens could also mean that they have intestinal worms, which rob chickens of nutrients. This can also be treated with medication. Sick chickens should be quarantined in a separate coop until they are better so that they do not infect the flock.

GROOMING YOUR CHICKENS

Sometimes chickens' nails, beaks, and feathers need trimming. Usually their toenails wear down from walking around. But some chickens develop long nails. You can trim them with dog nail clippers. You may want someone to hold the hen securely while you trim. Chickens have veins in their nails, which will bleed if you cut the nails too deeply. Clip only enough so that the hen can walk comfortably. If you see the nail change color on the inside, stop clipping, as you are close to the vein. Some hens' beaks also grow faster than others. If they are not worn down by pecking at chicken scratch, they can overlap and make it awkward for the chickens to eat. You can either trim them slightly with clippers or file the beaks with a nail file. Finally, its best to leave your hens' feathers intact, and most chickens don't fly very well. However, if your chicken is a talented flyer (and has a talent for getting into trouble,) you can trim its wings for its own safety (so that it doesn't wind up in a dog's yard or get hit by a car). Wait until the feathers have come fully in. Then clip the main feathers, that is, the long feathers at the top of the wings. Trim them so that they are even with the rest of the feathers on the wing.

PREDATORS

We've talked briefly about safety from predators. The first line of defense is to keep chickens in a secure coop at night and in the early evening, when animals hunt. If crafty predators "break in" to the coop, use noise to scare them away. During the day, secure your chicken run with fencing. You may also consider a chicken guard dog. If neighborhood dogs or cats prey on your chickens, talk to their owners, or if they are strays, call animal control. As for wild animals, you may be limited in what you can do. You can set rat traps, but other wild animals, such as hawks,

Depending on their temperament, pets can be helpful or harmful to chickens. Cats can keep away rodents. But they may also prey on the chickens themselves.

owls, and coyotes, may be protected. However, your local wild-life services branch may agree to move wild animals that have killed chickens.

With proper care and a little luck, chickens typically live to be about ten years old. Over the years, you'll come to know their unique personalities and appreciate them for their companion-ship and food. You'll also develop confidence and self-sufficiency and will probably learn to make a mean omelet.

GLOSSARY

BROODY The quality of sitting on eggs, fertilized or not, which some hens display as part of their maternal instincts.

CHICK A newborn or young chicken or other bird. Chickens are considered chicks until they grow their scapular feathers.

COOP A house for chickens that is designed to protect them from predators, provide shelter, and allow a quiet nest in which to lay eggs.

DOCILE The quality of being calm, desirable in domesticated animals so that they can be managed and handled by their owners.

FEED A mixture of grains that comprises the main food that chickens eat.

FERTILIZER A substance, often rich in nitrogen, that promotes growth in plants. Chicken manure is one example.

FIRST EGGS The small eggs that hens lay when they first reach laying age.

FLIGHTY The quality of flying off that some chickens display.

FORAGE To search for food, either growing in the wild or in a yard.

FOWL Birds prized for their eggs and meat.

FREE RANGE Being allowed to roam freely in a yard or pasture for much of the day.

HEIRLOOM CHICKEN A rare breed of chicken that was more common in the past.

HEN A female chicken or other fowl.

JUNGLE FOWL The wild breed of birds, living in Asia and the Pacific, from which the domesticated chicken originates.

LAYER A domesticated bird raised for its eggs.

POULTRY Domesticated fowl.

PREDATOR An animal that hunts and eats other animals.

PULLET A female chick that has developed its scapular (shoulder) feathers and is less than one year old.

ROOSTER A male chicken.

RUN An enclosed outdoor space in which chickens can forage or peck.

SCRATCH A snack feed, comprised of seeds, cornmeal, and other ingredients, scattered on the ground for chickens.

URBAN FARM A farm in the city.

VENT The opening through which birds lay eggs and eliminate waste.

The American Livestock Breeds Conservancy
P.O. Box 477
Pittsboro, NC 27312
(919) 542-5704
Web site: http://www.albc-usa.org
The American Livestock Breeds Conservancy protects
   threatened breeds of domesticated animals from going
   extinct.

American Pastured Poultry Producers Association
P.O. Box 85
Hughesville, PA 17737-0085
(570) 584-2309
Web site: http://www.apppa.org
The American Pastured Poultry Producers Association is a non-
   profit educational and networking group for free-range chicken
   farmers.

American Poultry Association
P.O. Box 306
Burgettstown, PA 15021
(724) 729-3459
Web site: http://www.amerpoultryassn.com
The American Poultry Association is dedicated to upholding
   the standards of breeds through education and shows.

4-H
7100 Connecticut Avenue
Chevy Chase, MD 20815
Web site: http://www.4-H.org
4-H is a youth-development organization focused on science,
    citizenship, and healthy living.

4-H Canada
Central Experimental Farm
960 Carling Avenue
Building 26
Ottawa, ON K1A 0C6
Canada
(613) 234-4448
Web site: http://www.4-h-canada.ca
4-H Canada is a youth development organization in Canada.

Future Farmers of America
P.O. Box 68960
6060 FFA Drive
Indianapolis, IN 46268-096
(317) 802-6060
Web site: http://www.ffa.org
The Future Farmers of America prepares young people for
    farming careers.

Rare Breeds Canada
2495 Boulevard Perrot
N.D. De L'Ile Perrot, QC J7V 8P4
Canada
Web site: http://www.rarebreedscanada.ca
Rare Breeds Canada is dedicated to the conservation of rare or
   endangered Canadian farm animals, including poultry.

WEB SITES

Due to the changing nature of Internet links, Rosen Publishing
has developed an online list of Web sites related to the subject
of this book. This site is updated regularly. Please use this link
to access the list:

http://www.rosenlinks.com/UGFT/Rais

FOR FURTHER READING

Alexander, Jill. *The Sweetheart of Prosper County.* New York, NY: Feiwel and Friends, 2009.

Backyardchickens.com members. *Backyard Chickens' Guide to Coops and Tractors: Planning, Building, and Real-Life Advice.* Blue Ash, OH: Betterway Home, 2011.

Bell, Kathleen Davitt. *Little Blog on the Prairie.* New York, NY: Bloomsbury USA, 2010.

Bloom, Jessi, and Kate Baldwin. *Free-Range Chicken Gardens: How to Create a Beautiful, Chicken-Friendly Yard.* Portland, OR: Timber Press, 2012.

Damerow, Gail. *The Chicken Encyclopedia: An Illustrated Reference.* North Adams, MA: Storey, 2012.

Ekarius, Carol. *Storey's Illustrated Guide to Poultry Breeds.* North Adams, MA: Storey, 2007.

English, Ashley. *Homemade Living: Keeping Chickens with Ashley English: All You Need to Know to Care for a Happy, Healthy Flock.* New York, NY: Lark Books, 2010.

Foreman, Patricia. *City Chicks: Keeping Micro-flocks of Chickens as Garden Helpers, Compost Makers, Bio-reyclers, and Local Food Producers.* Buena Vista, VA: Good Earth Publications, 2010.

Gleason, Chris. *Art of the Chicken Coop: A Fun and Essential Guide to Housing Your Peeps.* East Petersburg, PA: Fox Chapel Publishing, 2011.

Heinrichs, Christine. *How to Raise Chickens: Everything You Need to Know.* McGregor, MN: Voyageur Press, 2007.

Kindschi, Tara. *4-H Guide to Raising Chickens.* McGregor, MN: Voyageur Press, 2010.

Langlois, Cherie. *Ducks: Tending a Small-Scale Flock for Pleasure and Profit.* Mission Viejo, CA: Hobby Farms, 2008.

Litt, Robert, and Hannah Litt. *A Chicken in Every Yard: The Urban Farm Store's Guide to Chicken Keeping.* Berkeley, CA: Ten Speed Press, 2011.

Luttmann, Rick, and Gail Luttmann. *Chickens in Your Backyard: A Beginner's Guide.* Emmaus, PA: Rodale Books, 1976.

Madigan, Carleen. *The Backyard Homestead: Produce All the Food You Need on Just a Quarter Acre!* North Adams, MA: Storey, 2009.

Pangman, Judy. *Chicken Coops: 45 Building Ideas for Housing Your Flock.* North Adams, MA: Storey, 2006.

Van Draanen, Wendelin. *Flipped.* New York, NY: Random House, 2003.

Weaver, Sue. *Chickens: Tending a Small-Scale Flock for Pleasure and Profit.* Mission Viejo, CA: Hobby Farms, 2005.

"America's 'Food Deserts.'" The Week, August 12, 2011.
Retrieved Jan. 15, 2013 (http://theweek.com/article/
index/218167/americarsquos-food-deserts).

Backyard Chickens. "Help! Pasty Butt." Retrieved February
15, 2013 (http://www.backyardchickens.com/t/827/
help-pasty-butt).

Backyard Farming. "Backyard Chickens: Molting." October 6,
2009. Retrieved February 10, 2013 (http://backyardfarming
.blogspot.com/2009/10/backyard-chickens-molting.html).

Block, Ben. "U.S. City Dwellers Flock to Raising Chickens."
World Watch Institute. Retrieved January 16, 2013 (http://
www.worldwatch.org/node/5900).

City Girl Chickens. "Chicken Egg Problems." Retrieved
February 10, 2013 (http://www.citygirlchickens.com/
chicken_egg_problems.html).

Damerow, Gail. *Storey's Guide to Raising Chickens.* North
Adams, MA: Storey, 2010.

Fimrite, Peter. "Children Detach from Natural World as They
Explore the Virtual One." *San Francisco Chronicle.* October
21, 2007. Retrieved January 16, 2013 (http://www.sfgate.
com/outdoors/article/Children-detach-from-natural-world
-as-they-2495482.php#ixzz2LHjstJn7).

Grebenc, Shelby. "Feeling Grateful Yet? Teenage Poultry
Farmer Dishes Straight Talk." *Denver Post*, November 10,
2010. Retrieved January 21, 2013 (http://www.denverpost
.com/recommended/ci_21967690).

Illinois Department of Public Health. "Human Health Concerns About Raising Poultry." March 2012. Retrieved February2013http://www.idph.state.il.us/health/infect/Poultry.html).

James, Marie. "Interesting Facts About Chicken Eggs." Backyard Chickens. March 16, 2012. Retrieved February 10, 2013 (http://www.backyardchickens.com/a/interesting-facts-about-chicken-eggs).

Megyesi, Jennifer. *The Joy of Keeping Chickens: The Ultimate Guide to Raising Poultry for Fun or Profit.* New York, NY: Skyhorse, 2009.

Moore, Alanna. *Backyard Poultry Naturally: A Complete Guide to Raising Chickens & Ducks Naturally.* Austin, TX: Acres USA, 2007.

Pfund, Emily. "Saginaw County Teens to Donate 1,000 Pounds of Chicken to Soup Kitchen After Fair." M Live, July 27, 2012. Retrieved January 21, 2013 (http://www.mlive.com/news/saginaw/index.ssf/2012/07/saginaw_county_teens_to_donate.html).

Price, Catherine. "A Chicken on Every Plot, a Coop in Every Backyard." *New York Times*, September 19, 2007. Retrieved January 15, 2013 (http://www.nytimes.com/2007/09/19/dining/19yard.html?pagewanted=all&_r=0).

Siebert, Charles. "Food Ark: Heirloom Breeds." *National Geographic*, July 2011. Retrieved February 10, 2013

(http://ngm.nationalgeographic.com/2011/07/food-ark/
heirloom-chickens#/6).

Smith, Kathie. "Raising Chickens Helps Teens Build Life
Skills." *Toledo Blade*, November 15, 2009. Retrieved
January 21, 2013 (http://www.toledoblade.com/
Food/2009/11/15/Raising-chickens-helps-teens-build
-life-skills.html).

University of Connecticut. "Fact Sheet: Poultry Diseases &
Medications for Small Flocks." Retrieved February 11,
2013 (http://web.uconn.edu/poultry/poultrypages/
diseasefactsheet.html).

Ussery, Harvey. *The Small-Scale Poultry Flock.* White River
Junction, VT: Chelsea Green Publishing, 2011.

Wallace, Lisa. "4-H Clubs Flourish with Crop of Urban
Locavores." *San Francisco Chronicle.* August 14, 2011.
Retrieved January 15, 2013 (http://www.sfgate.com/
homeandgarden/article/4-H-clubs-flourish-with-crop-of
-urban-locavores-2335566.php#ixzz2LHiG8emr).

Woginrich, Jenna. *Chick Days: Raising Chickens from
Hatchlings to Laying Hens.* North Adams, MA: Storey
Publishing, 2010.

INDEX

ABOUT THE AUTHOR

Bridget Heos is the author of more than fifty books for kids and teens. She lives in Kansas City with her husband and four children. As a child, she was an avid gardener.

PHOTO CREDITS

Cover © iStockphoto.com/SimplyCreativePhotography; p. 5 Boston Globe/Getty Images; pp. 8–9 FPG/Archive Photos/Getty Images; p. 11 The Washington Post/Getty Images; pp. 14–15 J.B Nicholas/Splash News/Newscom; pp. 18, 40 © AP Images; p. 21 © Lee Beel/Alamy; p. 23 Natasha K/Botanica/Getty Images; pp. 26–27, 51 iStockphoto/Thinkstock; pp. 28–29 Rene Morris/ Taxi/Getty Images; p. 32 © Peter Hvizdak/The Image Works; p. 34 © iStockphoto.com/Tobias Helbig; pp. 36–37 Dougal Waters/Digital Vision/Getty Images; p. 43 Philippe Henry/First Light/Getty Images; p. 45 Universal Images Group/Getty Images; p. 48 © iStockphoto.com/Kary Nieuwenhuis; cover and interior pages (cityscape silhouette) © iStockphoto.com/blackred; cover and interior pages (dirt) © iStockphoto.com/wragg; back cover (chickens silhouette) © iStockphoto.com/davidnay.

Designer: Nicole Russo; Editor: Bethany Bryan; Photo Researcher: Amy Feinberg